W9-BLV-379

VALENTINE

50 Years of Celebrating Life's Most Treasured Moments

Vol. 51, No. 1

Publisher, Patricia A. Pingry
Associate Editor, Lisa C. Thompson
Art Director, Patrick McRae
Contributing Editors, Lansing Christman, Deana Deck, Russ Flint, Pamela Kennedy, Heidi King, Nancy Skarmeas
Editorial Assistant, Laura Matter

ISBN 0-8249-1114-8

IDEALS—Vol. 51, No. 1 February MCMXCIV IDEALS (ISSN 0019-137X) is published eight times a year: February, March, May, June, August, September, November, December by IDEALS PUBLICATIONS INCORPORATED, 565 Marriott Drive, Nashville, TN 37214. Second-class postage paid at Nashville, Tennessee, and additional mailing offices. Copyright © MCMXCIV by IDEALS PUBLICATIONS INCORPORATED. POSTMASTER: Send address changes to Ideals, PO Box 148000, Nashville, TN 37214-8000. All rights reserved. Title IDEALS registered U.S. Patent Office.

SINGLE ISSUE—$4.95
ONE-YEAR SUBSCRIPTION—eight consecutive issues as published—$19.95
TWO-YEAR SUBSCRIPTION—sixteen consecutive issues as published—$35.95
Outside U.S.A., add $6.00 per subscription year for postage and handling.

ACKNOWLEDGMENTS

FATHER GIVES HIS VERSION by Edgar A. Guest from HARBOR LIGHTS OF HOME, copyright ©1928 by The Reilly & Lee Co. Used by permission of the author's estate. FEBRUARY from THE GOLDEN ROAD by Edna Jaques, published in Canada by Thomas Allen & Son Limited. THE SURPRISE from ROSES FOR REMEMBRANCE by Patience Strong. Copyright 1960 by Patience Strong, published by Frederick Muller Ltd. Reprinted by permission of Rupert Crew Limited. Our Sincere Thanks to the following authors whom we were unable to contact: Grace E. Bayne for FOOTPRINTS OF LOVE; Patricia Ann Emme for BECAUSE OF YOUR LOVE; Vera Hardman for ON WINGS OF LOVE; Rosa Zagnoni Marinoni for LOVE IS A LITTLE CHURCH; Leonard G. Nattkemper for WINTERTIME; Celia Uhrman for OH, MY DARLING; and Eleanor Graham Vance for COMPASS.

Four-color separations by Precision Color Graphics Ltd., New Berlin, Wisconsin.

Printing by The Banta Company, Menasha, Wisconsin. Printed on Weyerhauser Husky.

The paper used in this publication meets the minimum requirements of American National Standard for Information Sciences—Permanence of Paper for Printed Library Materials, ANSI Z39.48-1984.

Unsolicited manuscripts will not be returned without a self-addressed stamped envelope.

Cover Photo
Obrien & Mayor/FPG

Inside Covers
Jerry Koser

Wintertime

Leonard G. Nattkemper

It seems I love the wintertime the best,
When all the growing things have stopped to rest.
For there's a mystery in silent snow,
And there's a tang in icy winds that blow.

And when I see the snowdrifts on the trees,
Where bloomed the flowers in spring for honeybees,
Old wrongs and hatreds melt, and worries cease;
The alchemy of winter's snow is peace.

When sleeping earth is blanketed with snow,
Then ev'ry seed of fruit and bloom below
Is dreaming of the blossom time of spring—
All set to music when the robins sing.

I could hardly get along, I guess,
Without old winter's frosty, sparkling dress
On ev'ry little twig and blade of grass,
Just glist'ning out a welcome as I pass.

For when there's winter, spring will not delay;
The things we cherish most will come someday,
If fearlessly we breast the storms and smile
And, like old Mother Earth, just wait awhile.

SUNRISE ON MT. TOM
Yosemite National Forest, Sierra Nevada
Ed Cooper Photography

In Winter

Stella Craft Tremble

A coat of falling ermine snow
Envelops all the earth below,
While, overcast, a sky of gray
Proclaims a stormy, winter day.
If in the night there comes a storm,
We'll have our blankets snug and warm.

Out in the woods beneath the sod
Sweet bergamots and trilliums nod.
Unmindful of the winter chill,
They softly sleep upon the hill.
But soon will come the voice of Spring
To call and waken everything.

Till then, tucked gently in the ground
They softly sleep, all safe and sound.
God tempers storms and guards us all;
He knoweth when the sparrows fall.
Can we not trust His constant care,
Since God is present everywhere?

Crimson Wings in Flight

Betty Harper Rohr

One eve as I was walking
　　Through meadows white and cold,
I came upon a big oak tree
　　With branches gnarled and old.

The snow like frosted silver clung
　　To frozen leafless limbs,
And there, bright as a ruby,
　　A red bird sang its hymns.

Its notes filled the frosted air
　　And held me in a trance,
While wisps of snow around me swirled
　　And with the wind did dance.

Then in a flash of color
　　On crimson wings in flight,
It soared into the sunset
　　And disappeared from sight.

NORTHERN CARDINAL, MALE
Adam Jones

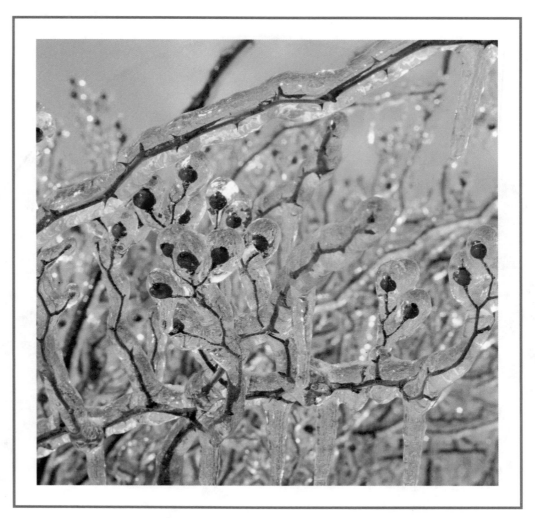

February

Edna Jaques

The fields are bedded down with snow,
Like blankets tucked about their ears,
As if the world had gone to sleep;
But now and then a bush appears,
Wearing a crown of purest gems
With scarlet berries on white stems.

The windbreak running to the lake
Has snowy trunks like silver birch.
Even the weeds have hoods of snow,
Like quaint old women in a church.

ICE TREE
Gene Ahrens
FPG International

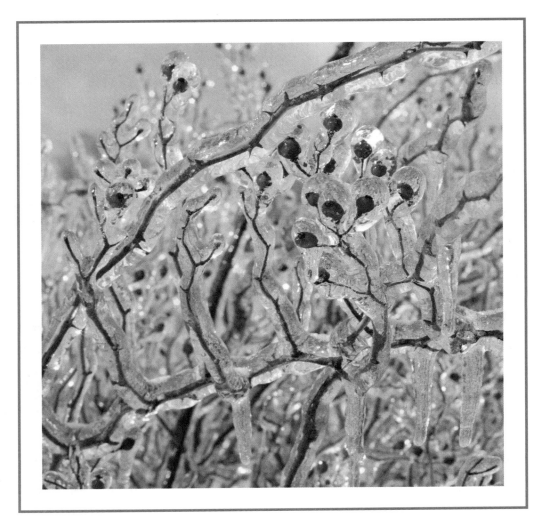

The hens have frosted beards and look
Like old men in a picture book.

Along the highway muffled wheels
Go by without a breath of sound.
The fence posts stand like sentinels,
Wearing tall helmets diamond crowned.
The mailman in his battered truck
Has drifted snow and ice to buck.

And yet I know that spring is nigh
Although the wind is cold and raw;
The sky is softer than it was;
The fields have started in to thaw,
Putting aside their winter dress
To don their springtime loveliness.

Country CHRONICLE

Lansing Christman

Young or old, we all like valentines. Here I am, well along in my years as an octogenarian, and valentines still brighten and lift my spirits. In this phase of my life, my valentines come from dear and compassionate friends. And the day seems so much sunnier and so much kinder when I receive a valentine.

This year, there was a special valentine for me from nature. When I awoke and looked out the window, I discovered a whole new world outside the door. The night had left a heavy white frost upon the land which covered shrubbery and grass—every blade and leaf, every spear and spire.

I did not take my usual morning walk. I did not want to mar the beautiful whiteness covering our pastures and fields, our dooryard and garden. For this brief moment, my world was one of loveliness. It was a morning of sheer perfection and charm.

There was beauty too in blossom and birdsong. Daffodils were in bloom as were snowdrops and violets and forsythias. And there were the birdsongs—the warbles of bluebirds and carols of robins, the crooning of the doves, the drumming of woodpeckers, and the songs of chickadees and cardinals. I listened to the chirps of the finches at the bird feeders in the yard—the house finch, the purple finch, and the gold finch.

When the first rays of the sun rose over the eastern hills, the land was cloaked in God's glory of morning and filled with sparkling jewels.

My countryside on Valentine's Day was one of frost and bloom and song. I found the frost

10

suggestive of a gracious white-haired lady wearing a tiara of loveliness that does not disappear with the coming of the new day's sun. Hers is a crown that will endure forever in my heart and dreams, for she too is a special valentine.

The author of two published books, Lansing Christman has been contributing to Ideals *for over twenty years. Mr. Christman has also been published in several American, foreign, and braille anthologies. He lives in rural South Carolina.*

WINTER IN NEW ENGLAND
Concord, Massachusetts
Dianne Dietrich Leis Photography

Love Is a Little Church

Rosa Zagnoni Marinoni

Love is a little church
Standing near a grove,
Warmed in winter days
By an old-fashioned stove;

The pews are plain and rustic,
The windows crude and small,
But through them you can see
The rain and snowflakes fall,

While in the warm interior
Familiar voices sing
And unseen angels circle
Above you, wing to wing!

Footprints of Love

Grace E. Bayne

Soft beams of moonlight,
Snow-covered hills,
A brilliant blue sky,
Bright daffodils,

A mockingbird's song,
An owl in flight—
These little things bring me
Such delight.

The love of a good man,
A fire on the hearth,
Falling raindrops
On tender earth,

A mountain tinged purple,
A calm blue sea,
Acorns falling
From a mighty oak tree,

The smell of smoke rising
From chimneys on high,
Making its way
To clouds in the sky,

And stars shining brightly
From heaven above
Leave on my heart
Footprints of love.

BE MY
VALENTINE

Readers' Reflections

A Rose

I watch the dew form on a rose
Upon this starlit night.
A rose I'll pick in the morn
While the sun is rising bright.

This rose I'll give to you with love
When our lips again shall meet.
For like the dew upon the rose,
Your kisses taste as sweet.

Randell DesPres
Frederick, Maryland

My Valentine

I looked the counter over,
I searched the verses through,
But I couldn't find a single card
That expressed my love for you.

So I take my pen in hand
And try to make you see
That you're a special valentine
That God has made for me.

He took a load of sweetness
And kindness full of smiles;
He sprinkled it with poise and grace
And made a lovely child.

She grew to be my lady fair,
So sweet and so refined.
With all my heart, I thank you, God,
For such a valentine.

Jim Powell
Montgomery, Alabama

Gramma's Roses

Whenever I see roses,
My Gramma I recall,
And the tender care and love
She showered on them all:

Red roses by the porch,
Tea roses by the door,
Yellow roses by the gate,
And in the backyard many more.

Simple was their beauty,
Their fragrance filled the air,
And the roses grew and thrived
Because of Gramma's loving care.

Carol Ellefson
Buffalo, Minnesota

Small Valentines

Something sticky this way comes;
I feel the prickling in my thumbs,
Syrupy verse or even worse,
Chocolate, waxed and runny.

Something sticky this way comes
With tattered lace or grimy crumbs,
Elastic sweets or homemade treats,
Hidden in a pocket.

Something sticky this way comes,
Love smeared with candied mediums,
A tiny face, where one can trace
Uncomplicated giving.

Elizabeth R. Crummer
Coeur d'Alene, Idaho

Editor's Note: Readers are invited to submit unpublished, original poetry for possible publication in future issues of *Ideals*. Please send copies only; manuscripts will not be returned. Writers receive $10 for each published submission. Send material to "Readers' Reflections," Ideals Publications Incorporated, P.O. Box 148000, Nashville, Tennessee 37214-8000.

First Love

Charles P. Isley

Sometimes in solitude I run
Back through the years so swiftly spun,

And from the mist of memory,
My first love comes again to me—

A phantom maiden, free of care,
With April tangled in her hair.

I feel her close; I know her lips,
The tender touch of fingertips,

The sandy beach, the water swell—
Her laughter that I knew so well,

The pain that hovered in my heart
When our two lives were split apart.

And then, as sudden as she came,
She leaves me to my own again.

Flowers in a Diary

Harriet C. Whipple

The book was old and dusty
When she found it on a shelf,
Long forgotten in the attic
Where she'd hidden it herself.

It was just a little diary
She had started years ago,
Telling all her hopes and fears
About a special beau.

It was at the high school picnic
(As she wrote it in her book)
That they wandered through the meadow
To the woods beyond the brook.

There he picked a spray of blossoms
That he fastened in her hair,
And then he kissed her shyly;
She was very young and fair.

They talked about the future
That seemed so far away,
And they made a secret promise
To be wed some happy day.

Then she pressed his pretty flowers
In her diary book that night
And wrote about her loved one
With eyes all shining bright.

Their lives took different pathways
With another love for each,
For one was born to wander
And the other born to teach.

The long forgotten diary
And the fragile flower spray
Revived some precious memories
Of a happy, youthful day.

COLLECTOR'S CORNER

Lisa C. Thompson

**Dancing is delightful
to the music of the Victrola**

Every one enjoys dancing to music of such splendid volume, such clearness and perfect rhythm and the Victrola plays as long as any one wants to dance.

The Victrola brings to you all kinds of music and entertainment, superbly rendered by the world's greatest artists who make records exclusively for the Victor.

Any Victor dealer will gladly play the latest dance music or any other music you wish to hear. There are Victors and Victrolas in great variety of styles from $10 to $200.

Victor Talking Machine Co., Camden, N. J., U. S. A.

1914 advertisement for the Victrola, manufactured by the Victor Talking Machine Company.

Victrolas

At the turn of the century, America fell in love with the phonograph. But while this new form of home entertainment took the country by storm, the appearance of the instrument met with some derision. Many people wanted something more elegant to display in their parlors. In 1906, Eldridge R. Johnson, founder of the Victor Talking Machine Company, introduced the Victrola—a phonograph whose mechanics, including the horn, were completely concealed within a four-foot-high mahogany cabinet. The Victrola was designed to look like a beautiful piece of furniture; and despite its two-hundred-dollar price tag, America bought it by the thousands.

The Victrola became so popular, in fact, that through the years the name Victrola became synonymous with phonograph and gramophone. In the early 1900s, however, the three terms had distinct meanings. The phonograph employed vertical-cut cylinders whereas the gramophone used lateral-cut discs. The Victrola brand was actually an enclosed gramophone. Eventually, the public dropped the term gramophone and used phonograph or Victrola to refer to any "talking machine."

Thomas Alva Edison invented the first "talking machine" in 1877. With his shouted words "Mary had a little lamb," a new era in home entertainment was born. Edison designed the

Parlor Speaking Phonograph, a crude apparatus using tin foil wrapped around a cylinder, and sold it for ten dollars. Public interest soon waned with the novelty, and Edison abandoned it for a different project—electric light.

Ten years later a German immigrant named Emile Berliner invented the first gramophone, which was an improved version of the phonograph and used lateral-cut discs instead of vertical-cut cylinders.

Another decade later, a twenty-nine-year-old mechanic in Camden, New Jersey, named Eldridge R. Johnson developed the Improved Gramophone. When legal battles with Berliner prevented him from using the name "gramophone," he chose Victor. But royalties still went to the owner of the gramophone patent—Berliner. Johnson proposed a merger with Berliner; and in 1901, the Victor Talking Machine Company was born.

The Victor Company enjoyed a huge success with the Victrola. Customers could choose from a range of sizes, prices, wood finishes, and cabinet designs, including custom-made, hand-painted cabinets. But the public soon tired of the squat-hinged lid on the Victrola and wanted period flat-topped cabinets of the eighteenth-century style. Johnson despised the flat-topped cabinets and resisted the trend; but when loyal Victrola customers pleaded, Johnson compromised. He designed a "flat-topped" Victrola with a raised portion in the center of the lid that covered the phonograph mechanism. Johnson did not want the Victrola used as a table. Quickly dubbed "the humpback," the new Victrola was played in very few American homes.

In 1922 the radio boom captured the public's attention. Victor's competitors quickly developed combination phonograph-radios and successfully capitalized on the new invention. But Johnson dismissed radio as insignificant. Finally in autumn of 1923, Johnson manufactured console Victrolas that included an empty compartment to be filled with the radio receiver of the customer's choosing. The new model Victrolas also included another feature that was conspicuously not advertised—the lid was finally flat.

Recording became electric in 1925, and on November 2, Victor introduced its new Orthophonic Victrola, which included RCA's radiola and a new phonograph that would play the improved electric recordings. November 2 was pronounced Victor Day by the company, and it was accompanied by the largest advertising campaign in Victor's history. The strategy worked: America began buying Victrolas again.

By 1926, Victor introduced its most expensive Victrola: the Borgia II for $1,000. The Borgia II included RCA's radiola as well as Victor's new Electrola, an all-electric record player. Customers began placing orders immediately, and the demand was so great that the plant in Camden fell behind on deliveries.

Johnson's health declined as he grew older, and he began to pay more attention to the offers he received to buy the company. In December of 1926, he sold Victor to J. & W. Seligman & Co. and Speyer & Co. Seligman and Speyer then sold Victor to RCA in January of 1929. Soon Camden was producing radio sets, and the company became the RCA Victor Division of the Radio Corporation of America.

The Victrola symbolizes an era in American history rich in innovation and prosperity. But collectors must be wary: not all disc phonographs with concealed horns are authentic Victrolas. Always check under the lid for the familiar Victrola trademark of the dog Nipper listening to "His Master's Voice."

In "His Master's Voice," painted by Francis Barraud, the dog Nipper is looking into a 1901 Type B Victor Talking Machine. The painting became a trademark of the Victor Talking Machine Company.

My Love for You

Harold F. Mohn

A rose will bloom then wither,
Its petals fall away,
Unlike the love I have for you
That thrives and grows each day.

A dream lasts only seconds
And then is gone and o'er,
Unlike the love I have for you
That will last evermore.

The waves wash in upon the beach,
Sand castles wash away,
Unlike the love I have for you
Most steadfast day by day.

The seasons come, the seasons go,
As they are bound to do,
Unlike the love within my heart
That lives each day anew.

PORTLAND HEAD LIGHTHOUSE
Cape Elizabeth, Maine
Johnson's Photography

My Valentine Wish

Kay Hoffman

I'd like to hang a valentine
Upon the world's front door,
With hearts of love and peace entwined
To last forevermore.

With love to guide our daily path,
There'd be no one in need;
God's blessings would be shared by all
Of every race and creed.

Peace would come to all the world
As nations great and small
Would put aside their selfish aims
To work for the good of all.

If I could have my wish today,
I'd wish for nothing more
Than to hang a great big valentine
Upon our world's front door.

To My Son, with Love

Philosophers discourse about the elevating aspects of love. Psychologists teach about its healing power. Romantics wax poetic and lovers become incoherent when asked to describe love's effects. But I have learned much of what I know about love from you, my eldest child, and the lessons have not always been easy.

I can recall with vivid detail love's wonder as your father and I stood in a tan cubicle of an office and were handed you, our first son. The adoption worker placed a chubby seven-week-old baby boy in my arms, and I felt love welling in my eyes. It was a love made intense through six long years of yearning. And after all that time, when finally I held you, the love I experienced was like the breaking of a dam—a flooding, rushing, tumbling mass of emotion, suddenly set free.

Within a few months I learned love was deeper and wider than I had ever imagined. It was unreasonable pride in accomplishments for

28

which I could claim no credit—a first smile, a first tooth, a first night slept through. Love, I also found, had a darker side that could surprise me with its raw intensity. Your raging fever whipped my love into frenzied fear, and imagined dangers stole my peaceful sleep. But all the while, love grew and changed me, shaping the contours of my life.

When you toddled out the door and into the sunny world, I ached with love at losing you to other people. You always returned for bandages, kisses, graham crackers, and clean clothes; but my love, I knew, would never again be sufficient for your needs. Other loves would push me out. Superheroes lured you away with promised power and magical tricks, and I could only offer songs and stories and hugs in the dark.

When someone stole your favorite toy, pushed you down, and called you ugly names, my love became an anger fierce as hate but was not strong enough to heal your wounds. Sometimes I could feel your little body refuse to give way to comfort in my arms, and my love felt weak and useless.

In school, when teachers looked at you with clear, dispassionate eyes and pointed out your weaknesses, my love wanted to argue, to give excuses for your missed answers and inattention. I longed to cover everything with love, to see things in a softer, kinder light.

As you grew, so did my love, but often it went undiscovered by your eyes. You saw it then as a barrier keeping out the bright and tantalizing freedom you desired. Long before, in a rush of childish adoration, you told me that you would marry only me; but later I became the enemy, guarding the doors to adventure, spoiling all your fun.

Adolescence somehow made love unintelligible. We were like strangers walking out of step in a foreign land. My love became clumsy, stilted, constantly misinterpreted—a frustrating and unrelenting companion. Now and then, however, like sun rays through the clouds, love would break in on us with blinding clarity; I carried those moments to cherish on the darker days. I know you felt it too, and, lost as I, you struggled

with your feelings. Caught between being a boy and becoming a man, you were in uncharted waters and could not risk becoming vulnerable to a mother's love.

I don't recall when things began to turn again, when slowly, haltingly, we began to relearn the same language. There was a day you let me hug you and you did not draw away. There was an afternoon when you brought me a funny card and tousled my hair and sat down beside me and we actually had a conversation. Like dancers learning to move in time together, we gingerly, tentatively made our way. Sometimes we stumbled or tread on one another's toes, but the steps came easier and surer day by day.

And now, you are going out the door again. Only this time you won't be toddling back in for graham crackers and stories. You won't come running with skinned knees to bandage and butterflies to admire. You are leaving home to find your place in the world, and my love is wondering if it can stretch that far.

I have learned much about love in these past eighteen years. I have found it has a will of its own and cannot always be contained by reasonable thought. I have discovered it is deeper, stronger, more resilient than I ever could have dreamed. I now know it will be with me like an unrelenting friend, peeking at me from behind memories and favorite places, coming unbidden in scents and sounds long after you have left my arms. You have stretched me and bent me in ways that have made me both weak and strong. I am a different person from the woman who gazed at you with wonder almost two decades ago. This Valentine's Day, I thank you for teaching me what it is to truly love a child.

Pamela Kennedy is a free-lance writer of short stories, articles, essays, and children's books. Wife of a naval officer and mother of three children, she has made her home on both U.S. coasts and in Hawaii and currently resides in Washington, D.C. She draws her material from her own experiences and memories, adding bits of her imagination to create a story or mood.

SNOWFLAKES
Mary Mapes Dodge

Whenever a snowflake leaves the sky,
It turns and turns to say "Good-by!
Good-by, dear clouds, so cool and gray!"
Then lightly travels on its way.

And when a snowflake finds a tree,
"Good-day!" it says, "Good-day to thee!
Thou art so bare and lonely, dear,
I'll rest and call my comrades here."

But when a snowflake, brave and meek,
Lights on a rosy maiden's cheek,
It starts, "How warm and soft the day!
'Tis summer!" and it melts away.

The unique perspective of Russ Flint's artistic style has made him a favorite of Ideals *readers for many years. A resident of California and father of four, Russ Flint has illustrated a children's Bible and many other books.*

On Wings of Love

Vera Hardman

I plucked a fluffy snow-white cloud
  From out a sky of blue
And centered there a crimson rose
  Still kissed by morning dew.

Then I sprinkled it with sunbeams,
  Scented it with flowers,
And added bits of silver moonlight
  Filled with magic powers.

I tucked in caressing love songs
  Of all the springtime birds
And wove in happy memories
  Of loving, tender words.

From this beauty then I fashioned
  A valentine for you
And sent it winging on its way
  With all my love so true.

You Are

Donna Ann Radford

Sometimes you are a silhouette
In some recess of my mind,
A glowing, soft, sweet shadow,
Always gentle, always kind.

Sometimes you ride the crest of
Each wave of conscious thought
Or crash into my awareness
With sudden fierce onslaught.

If there be miles between us,
We are never far apart,
For you are always with me,
On my mind and in my heart.

34

BITS & PIECES

Love is giving freely, expecting nothing in return. Law concerns itself with an equitable exchange, *this for that*. Law is made necessary by people; love is made possible by God.
 Mary Carson

Life is just one fool thing after another; love is just two fool things after each other.
 Charles Reade

Who loves, raves—'tis youth's frenzy—
  but the cure is bitterer still.
  Lord Byron

Let no one who loves be called altogether unhappy. Even love unreturned has its rainbow.
  J. M. Barrie

It doesn't matter who you love or how you love but that you love.
 Rod McKuen

Oh, my darling, I love you so,
That words of love simply flow;
As I think of you all the time,
They simply pour out in rhyme,
Making a shower of love rain,
Which no power can restrain.
      Celia Uhrman

Love does not consist in gazing
at each other but in looking
together in the same direction.
      Antoine de Saint-Exupery

Do not the most moving
moments of our lives find
us all without words?
      Marcel Marceau

If yet I have not all thy love,
Dear, I shall never have it all.
      John Donne

Jenny kissed me when we met,
Jumping from the chair she sat in;
Time, you thief, who love to get
Sweets into your list, put that in:
Say I'm weary, say I'm sad,
Say that health and wealth have missed me,
Say I'm growing old, but add,
Jenny kissed me.
      Leigh Hunt

37

As I Am

Bill Carr

I'd like to give you everything
That wealth could ever buy—
Precious gems and golden rings
Or stars from up on high.

But since I do not have the wealth
To give these things to you,
You'll have to take me as I am,
And love will have to do.

YELLOW TIGER
Dick Dietrich Photography

Compass

Eleanor Graham Vance

A compass does not fly or sing;
It never ventures forth.
A compass is a constant thing:
It always points due north.

My thoughts are compass-like, I fear;
To one form they run true:
No matter how I guide them, dear,
They still return to you.

Love Words

Garnett Ann Schultz

The same words have been spoken
So many times before;
A million lips have used the phrase
"I love you" more and more.
It's still the same old promise
When two hearts say, "I do."
So many times before, I'm sure,
A kiss was shared by two.

The same old moon is shining;
The same old stars are there.
Somebody else has eyes of blue
And lovely shining hair.
Those love words sweet and precious,
So simple in their way,
That soft endearing "I love you"
Said long before this day,

So many times, but not the same,
So different from the start,
Three little words that mean the world
You told me with your heart.
Your lips have sealed the promise;
Your eyes have shown their love;
Your smile is like an angel's song
From heaven up above.

The same old words that lovers use,
And yet the thrill is new.
I've never heard them said before;
They've never been as true.
You picked them from the stars on high
And sprinkled them with dew
To bring me all I've dreamed about
In three words: "I love you."

Photo Opposite
MINIATURE ROSE "STARINA"
Barry L. Runk
Grant Heilman Photography

Lisa C. Thompson

Radio City Music Hall, New York, New York. Photograph courtesy of Radio City Music Hall Productions, Inc.

Radio City Music Hall
New York, New York

On December 27, 1932, Radio City Music Hall opened its doors for the first time. The opening night program featured nineteen variety acts, including the Radio City Music Hall Orchestra, the Radio City Music Hall Roxyettes (now known as the Rockettes), the Flying Wallendas, Ray Bolger, and Martha Graham. The producers had planned what they thought was a two-and-a-half-hour show, but the final bow wasn't taken until five hours after the show began. Reviewers criticized the variety format but praised the architectural design of the theater. Today, Radio City Music Hall is nick-named the "art deco palace of New York City."

The theater's design began as the dream of S. L. "Roxy" Rothafel, a successful theater producer and manager who ran the Roxy Theatre in New York City. While returning from a business trip to Europe, he witnessed a beautiful sunrise on the ocean. The sunrise design of the sixty-foot proscenium arch and ceiling in the Music Hall is a stylized interpretation of his vision.

The Music Hall promptly changed the show's format after that lengthy opening night. They instituted a new policy, effective immediately: no show on Radio City Music Hall's stage would ever run longer than fifty minutes, a policy in effect for forty-six years. Instead of variety acts, the Music Hall featured film debuts, beginning with *The Bitter Tea of General Yen*, starring Nils Asther and Barbara Stanwyck. Through the years, Radio City Music Hall featured the premieres of films such as *Little Women, National Velvet, Breakfast at Tiffany's,* and *Doctor Zhivago.* The last film presented at the Music Hall was *The Promise* in 1979.

One year before, talk of demolishing Radio City Music Hall stirred the public into action. Within a year, the Landmark Preservation Commission of the City of New York declared it a landmark, a designation stipulating all public areas of the theater be maintained in their original design, fabric, color, and style. In April of 1979, the meticulous restoration of the Music Hall began. Every piece of fabric was either replaced or restored, the bronze doors and marble pillars were polished, and even the twenty-four karat gold-leaf ceiling in the Grand Foyer was completely cleaned.

The "Behind-the-Scenes" tour of Radio City Music Hall takes visitors through the Grand Foyer, which stretches an entire city block and features two twenty-nine-foot chandeliers. The tour continues into the auditorium, where, if current productions permit, guests can actually walk across the 9,576-square-foot stage—the largest in the world. Visitors will also see the famous Mighty Wurlitzer, the largest theater organ in the world, and the costume shop where all of the costumes are created for Radio City productions. Another part of the tour is the vast underground hydraulic system that served as the prototype for the hydraulics on World War II aircraft carriers.

For many visitors, the highlight of the "Behind-the-Scenes" tour is meeting a Rockette. She'll discuss the history of the dance troupe, tell personal anecdotes, answer questions, and even pose for photographs.

The Radio City Music Hall Rockettes made their show business debut as the Missouri Rockets in St. Louis, Missouri, in 1925. Roxy

RADIO CITY MUSIC HALL ROCKETTES. Photograph by Eduardo Patino, courtesy of Radio City Music Hall Productions, Inc.

Rothafel discovered them and introduced them at his New York Roxy Theatre as the Roxyettes. Under the direction of their original creator and choreographer, Russell Markert, the Rockettes went on to make show business history as an integral part of Radio City Music Hall.

Markert worked with the Rockettes until his retirement in 1971. His concept of the dance line was absolutely uniform precision. While he choreographed intricate routines, his aim was always to keep the line moving as one. Everything was kept completely uniform—steps, costumes, and even height. The illusion of uniform height is maintained today by placing the tallest dancers in the center and gradually decreasing in height to both ends of the line.

While the Rockettes are internationally known as stars of Radio City Music Hall, they have also performed on the road. During World War II members of the Rockettes danced in USO tours throughout the world in support of our nation's armed forces.

Today, Radio City Music Hall is a premiere concert venue for top performers of popular music. In addition, thousands of people attend the special Christmas and Easter shows presented at the Music Hall every year.

Visitors to the "art deco palace of New York City" can take a walk through time in the restored Music Hall, interview a Rockette, or attend a dazzling show. A legend in the history of American film and music, Radio City Music Hall continues to entertain its guests in style.

LEGENDARY AMERICANS

Nancy Skarmeas

Cole Porter

Cole Porter liked to make songwriting look easy. The composer of such American classics as "Night and Day," "I Get a Kick Out of You," and "Anything Goes," Porter kept his creative process private. He never let friends and associates see him at work; he preferred to let them imagine that songs simply came to him in moments of inspiration. Rather than editing with a collaborator, a process he found painful, Porter would simply discard a song if it were not acceptable and start anew. He kept his well-worn rhyming dictionary well-hidden, preferring to maintain the popular perception that his witty, intelligent lyrics flowed freely from his pen. At the opening of his Broadway musicals, Porter was always conspicuously unconcerned, laughing and socializing as if the success of the show were the last thing on his mind.

In truth, it was the first and only thing on his mind—not success for its own sake, but as proof that the audience enjoyed his work. Cole Porter was a meticulous worker of considerable talents who poured his every effort into each song or musical that he wrote. To Porter, the greatest achievement to be dreamed of was to write a song that would be embraced by the American public as a "standard."

Perhaps this longing for public approval is what led Cole Porter to become a writer of popular songs in the first place, for he did not come to the career naturally by background or education. Born to wealth and privilege in Peru, Indiana, Porter had been classically trained as a musician and had studied at both Harvard and Yale. He had also spent several years in Paris as a student of the classicist Vincent d'Indy, learning orchestration and composition. One of Porter's first public works was an opera, which met with great success and seemed to be the start of a career as a classical composer. Porter was wealthy, educated, and often publically disdainful of what he considered more common forms of music written by popular composers such as Irving Berlin. At a time when the Great Depression had left so many Americans out of jobs and out of hope, Cole Porter seemed hopelessly out of touch with the common American and entirely disinterested in American popular music.

Yet, almost in spite of himself, Porter was drawn to the bright lights and the enthusiastic crowds of Broadway. Beginning in December of 1929 with the opening of *Wake Up and Dream*, Porter left his classical aspirations behind, devoted himself entirely to musical comedy, and wrote a string of hugely successful shows that pro-

duced an almost endless list of hit songs. Porter did not abandon his classical training; he simply put it to work in the format of the popular song. His elegant, sophisticated tunes, matched note for note with literate and intelligent lyrics, gave us shows like *Anything Goes* and *Gay Divorcé* featuring songs such as "Begin the Beguine," "You're the Top," and "It's De-Lovely," songs that gave a lift to the sagging spirits of Americans and international fame to their composer. His songs were unlike anything before them. They were complex and often difficult to play and sing, and their lyrics were entirely unsentimental. They were also irresistible. By the end of the decade, the name Cole Porter was synonymous with American popular music.

Yet, despite his success, Porter always felt the need to maintain his public air of ease and detachment; it was a well-practiced habit. In public he was forever the carefree man of wealth and education, even as in private he continued to work hard to produce great popular music. A tragic horseback riding accident in 1937 slowed Porter down considerably but did not put an end to his productivity. In 1948, while still suffering from the pain that would remain with him for the rest of his life, he wrote the songs for *Kiss Me Kate*, which is perhaps the best-loved of all his musicals.

Late in his life, Cole Porter learned that five of his songs had made an ASCAP listing of the top thirty American popular songs of all time. He could not have been happier. Although to his last days he retained a public reputation as a bit of a highbrow (who nonetheless wrote great popular songs), Cole Porter was, in truth, a man of the people. He understood that the value of a song is measured not by the education of the composer, but in how many people it amuses, uplifts, or enlightens. He craved public approval because he wanted his audience to take the same joy in songs that he did. At a time when so many Americans needed a lift and a diversion, Cole Porter gave them one in his own elegant, sophisticated, and detached way. Today, when we talk about the "American standards," we mean the work of Cole Porter.

Love Poem

Craig E. Sathoff

A gay corsage could speak for me;
Perhaps a note would do,
That states, in all simplicity,
"I am in love with you."

But that would not explain the way
I feel within my heart,
That though I've known you briefly, dear,
I never want to part.

You are the warmth of spring's return,
So gentle and so calm,
So lithe and full of gracefulness,
So filled with lovely charm.

I love the softness of your voice,
The shyness of your smile,
The tenderness within your eyes,
Your naturalness of style.

I feel whenever I'm with you
That there I, too, should stay
To love and share with you, my dear,
Each grand and hopeful day.

This is my poem of love for you,
And if you love me too,
You need not write a poem for me;
"I love you, too" will do.

46

Photo Opposite
RUSTIC COUNTRY LIVING
Jessie Walker Associates

A Bit of Love

Joyce Murphy

I caught a bit of love today
And put it in a jar,
But its fuzzy body wiggled free
And flew somewhere afar.

I smelled a bit of love today—
A tempting fragrance sweet—
A trace of mint and lilac,
Spring grass beneath my feet.

I touched some bits of love today;
I felt them with my hand—
Two mud pies, three smooth stones,
One castle made of sand.

I saw a bit of love today
When the golden sun set low
And covered every living thing
With its gentle twilight glow.

Opposite Page
MOUNT MCKINLEY
Denali National Park and Preserve, Alaska
Jeff Gnass Photography

The Forever Valentine

Jeanne Knape

I received my first valentine in third grade—from a boy. A boy with a crush on me. I was dazed.

The heart-shaped valentine covered my hands when I held it, it was so large. The brilliant red designs, accented with glitter and ornate lettering, professed of great, young love.

My heart throbbed while my face turned as red as the valentine. Someone liked me. Even as my classmates jeered, a certain thread of pride filled my heart. A boy noticed me.

I shoved the special card in my desk. Because of peer pressure I said, "Ugh, boys." The girls laughed, and the taunts from the boys grew louder.

There was only one problem with the card: it wasn't signed. The only hand-written words told of the author's devotion. I spent the day wondering who it was from. Could it be David, whose father was rich? Or Scott, with his good looks? Maybe it was the athletic Gerald, who could beat anyone on the track field.

After carefully carrying my special object home, I hid it in my dresser. While closing the drawer, I looked at myself in the mirror. My thin face and straight hair were reflected back at me. Why would any boy like me?

I spent the evening in a romantic haze. My mother had to tell me three times to come to supper, and my dad questioned my inattentiveness. I told no one at home about my card. I was afraid their reaction would be the same as my classmates'.

I wondered for weeks who my secret admirer was. He never revealed himself to me. I daydreamed about innocent encounters with the boy who liked me.

The end of the school year arrived before I finally found out who the mystery boy was, and even then it was only by accident. The handwriting etched in my mind jumped out at me one day when we exchanged papers during correction time. I held the paper of my secret boyfriend.

It was Paul. I hated Paul. He teased me, taunted me, and pulled my hair. Of course, what I didn't know then was that he did all these things to hide the fact that he liked me. Paul didn't want our classmates to know he had sent the card any more than I did.

But I still have that card. In fact, it's framed and hanging in my home. Is my husband jealous of my first love? Heavens no! I married Paul fifteen years after he sent that first valentine.

Photo Opposite
HANDMADE VALENTINE
Robert Barclay
Grant Heilman Photography

Handmade Heirloom

UNICORN by Ruthanne Kramer Hartung. Photograph by Michael Lauter, courtesy of Ruthanne Kramer Hartung.

Frakturs

Heidi King

Centuries ago, German folk artists began creating decorative certificates called frakturs to serve as pictorial records of family trees or important events in their lives, such as marriages, baptisms, and births. The genealogical information or special dates were hand-lettered on paper and decorated with small organic or geometric motifs. Today, the art of making frakturs is appreciated for its sentimental value and simple beauty.

When the art form was first introduced, no organized branch of government existed to keep track of important events. Consequently, people felt a need to record special dates in a tangible form as a remembrance and as a record for their children.

This time-honored practice can be traced to Renaissance Europe, where religious manuscripts were heavily decorated by monks. Monasteries were one of the few places where paper was available, and even then it was considered extremely precious. The monks would reproduce portions of the Bible and then decorate any remaining white space around the traditional Gothic lettering with ornate designs in a variety of colors. Jewish scholars also contributed a great deal to the practice by copying historical and religious manuscripts in a similar manner.

Later, as more people learned to read and write, creating frakturs became more widespread. Following the trend in furniture, pottery, and linens, the hand-lettering was embellished with designs and motifs. And because of the preciousness of paper, it was important to get as much decoration on the paper as possible.

In the seventeenth and eighteenth centuries, German immigrants brought the technique with them when they settled in Pennsylvania. German schoolteachers were called upon to draw certificates of baptism, marriage, and birth. Carpenters also began to use frakturs as a way to showcase their skills. They would develop a portfolio of colorful designs that could be carved into wood as samples to show customers. It was also around this time that blank certificates printed with designs and poems appeared. The names and dates of the event were all that had to be added to the paper.

Not all craftspeople who made frakturs were considered experts. Some of the oldest examples are illustrated with primitive drawings which were clearly done by novices. Many of the earlier artists worked in a freehand style, breaking words and simply continuing on the next line if needed. Most of the designs and decorations were also drawn freehand with ink. Today's fraktur artists often lightly draw the letters and designs to achieve balance and symmetry before actually applying the ink. Once the ink dries, color is added to the outlined designs.

Typically, frakturs are characterized by large angular shapes combined with colorful decorations. These are derived from gothic lettering, recognized by bulky characters written in black ink. Before the Revolutionary War, soldiers, horses, and crowns were drawn on many frakturs. After the war, the imperial designs were discarded in favor of tulips, hearts, and angels. Many of the decorations, such as animals, leaves, and flowers, are adapted from nature. Others are simple geometric shapes that can easily be mastered by a novice. Whereas recording important family dates was the primary reason for creating a fraktur, many designs have also included religious verses and poems.

HOUSE BLESSING by Ruthanne Kramer Hartung. Michael Lauter Photography.

Traditional frakturs adorned with religious symbols remain popular, but whimsical motifs and more relaxed lettering have come to characterize modern frakturs. Families often choose motifs that depict personal memories, milestones, and musings.

When making frakturs, a laid paper works well because of the way it holds the ink and watercolor. A variety of papers can be used, from handmade pulp papers to parchments. Today's frakturs are also decorated with inks in a spectrum of colors. For traditional frakturs, craftspeople use red and black inks, or if they wish to "age" a piece, a mellow brown will be used to imitate black ink faded with time. To achieve the strokes found in earlier frakturs, the smoothness of a ball-point pen is sacrificed in favor of feather quills.

The past twenty years have brought about a revival of the folk art of frakturs. In a society where "one size fits all," the personal messages and designs of frakturs are attractive, and since they can be created by an amateur, frakturs are a rewarding form of artistic expression.

Heidi King, a free-lance writer and designer, lives in Tallahassee, Florida.

A Valentine Box Was the Rule

Loise Pinkerton Fritz

On Valentine's Day my thoughts wend their way
    Back to the old village school,
Where Dan Cupid played his "Heart-Arrow" game,
    And a valentine box was the rule.

A discarded box with a slot in the top
    Was changed into beauty untold
With pasted red hearts, some verse from old cards,
    And lace, paper lace, white and gold.

At the old village store, for a penny, not more,
    We'd choose valentines we liked best;
We'd write "To" and "From" on most every one,
    Except those intended for jest.

Excitement was great on that special day
    When Teacher would open the box;
'Twas always my wish not one would be missed,
    For this was a day none forgot.

The years have marched on—they've come and they've gone—
    But still sits the old village school,
Where for Valentine's Day we scarcely could wait
    'Cause a valentine box was the rule.

A SLICE OF LIFE

— Edgar A. Guest —

Father Gives His Version

Well, you see, I met your mother
    at a wedding, long ago.
And though I was four-and-twenty,
    up to then I didn't know
That in all our busy city, which I'd
    traveled up and down,
There was such a lovely creature,
    with such lustrous eyes of brown.
But the minute that I saw her
    I just stared and stared and stared,
And right then I would have hugged her
    and kissed her—if I'd dared!

She was acting as the bridesmaid,
    I was best man for the groom,
And of course the bride was lovely,
    but the loveliest in the room
Wasn't just then getting married—
    'twas my thought as I stood there—
For I couldn't keep from staring
    at your mother, I declare.
And I couldn't keep from thinking,
    as we knelt there, side by side,
There must be another wedding,
    and then she must be my bride.

Well, the wedding party scattered,
    bride and groom and guests and all,
But I asked that lovely bridesmaid
    if she'd let me come to call.
Well, she blushed and gave permission,
    and when Sunday evening came,
I bought a box of candy,
    with a very famous name,
And I went up there to see her,
    and her Pa and Ma were there,
And I wanted *so* to kiss her—
    but of course I didn't dare.

Now that's how I met your mother—
    and 'twas twenty years ago,
And there was another wedding—
    just the one I'd longed to know,
For one lovely Sunday evening,
    when I went up there to call,
I caught her up and kissed her,
    as we lingered in the hall,

And we planned right then to marry—
    it was love that made me bold—
Now that's how I met your mother—
    but don't tell her that I told.

---

*Edgar A. Guest began his illustrious
career in 1895 at the age of fourteen
when his work first appeared in the*
Detroit Free Press. *His column was syn-
dicated in over 300 newspapers, and he
became known as "The Poet of the
People."*

57

To Celia

Ben Jonson

Drink to me only with thine eyes,
And I will pledge with mine;
Or leave a kiss but in the cup,
And I'll not look for wine.
The thirst that from the soul doth rise,
Doth ask a drink divine:
But might I of Jove's nectar sup,
I would not change for thine.

I sent thee late a rosy wreath,
Not so much honoring thee,
As giving it a hope, that there
It could not withered be.
But thou thereon did'st only breathe,
And sent'st it back to me;
Since when it grows and smells, I swear,
Not of itself, but thee.

Will You Love Me When I'm Old?

Author Unknown

I would ask of you, my darling,
A question, soft and low,
That gives me many a heartache
As the moments come and go.

Your love, I know, is truthful,
But the truest love grows cold;
It is this that I would ask you:
Will you love me when I'm old?

Life's morn will soon be waning,
And its evening bells shall toll,
But my heart shall know no sadness
If you'll love me when I'm old.

Down the stream of life together
We sail on side by side,
Hoping some bright day to anchor
Safe beyond its surging tide.

Today our sky is cloudless,
But the night may clouds unfold;
And though storms may gather round us,
Will you love me when I'm old?

When my hair shall shade the snowdrift
And mine eyes shall dimmer grow,
I would lean upon some loved one
Through the valley as I go.

I would claim of you a promise
Worth to me a world of gold;
It is only this, my darling,
That you'll love me when I'm old.

Kitchen Memo

D. A. Hoover

Make a little note of this;
Tack it to the wall;
Read it now and then each spring,
Summertime, and fall,
When the skies are overcast,
White with falling snow:
How I love you, and you are
The dearest one I know.
Anywhere we ever live
Shall be bright and warm,
Every happy day worthwhile,
Circled by your charm.

Ideals' Family Recipes

Favorite recipes from the *Ideals* family of readers.

Editor's Note: If you would like us to consider your favorite recipe, please send a typed copy of the recipe along with your name and address to *Ideals* Magazine, ATTN: Recipes, P.O. Box 148000, Nashville, Tennessee 37214-8000. We will pay $10 for each recipe used. Recipes cannot be returned.

FROZEN STRAWBERRY YUM YUM

In a large mixing bowl, combine 1 cup flour, ¼ cup packed brown sugar, ½ cup softened butter or margarine, and ¼ cup chopped walnuts. Blend until crumbly. Press into an 8 x 8-inch baking dish. Bake in a preheated 350° oven for about 20 to 24 minutes. Cool thoroughly. Break into crumbs. Sprinkle half of the crumb mixture evenly over the bottom of a 9 x 9-inch baking pan. Set aside.

In a large mixing bowl, combine 1 cup granulated sugar (less if berries are sweetened), one 10-ounce package frozen strawberries, 2 egg whites, and 2 teaspoons lemon juice. Beat at medium speed of electric mixer 15 to 20 minutes. Fold in one 12-ounce carton refrigerated whipped topping. Spread berry mixture over the crumbs in pan. Top with remaining crumbs. Freeze until ready to serve.

Mary Catherine Foust
Michigan City, Indiana

No-Bake Cheese Cake Dessert

In a small bowl, combine 2 cups graham cracker crumbs with ½ cup melted butter or margarine; mix well. Set aside ¾ cup of the crumb mixture; press remaining crumbs into a 9 x 13-inch pan. Freeze for at least 1 hour or refrigerate overnight.

In a large mixing bowl, combine one 8-ounce package softened cream cheese and 1 cup powdered sugar; beat until light. Stir in one 8-ounce carton refrigerated whipped topping, mixing thoroughly. Spread half of the cream cheese mixture over crumb crust. Pour one 20-ounce can cherry (or blueberry) pie filling over cream cheese and spread smoothly. Spread remaining cream cheese mixture over top. Sprinkle remaining crumbs over all. Refrigerate until ready to serve.

Mrs. Donald Rogers
Le Roy, Kansas

Fruit Pizza

In a large bowl, combine 1 cup margarine with 1½ cups powdered sugar; cream until light and fluffy. Add 2½ cups flour, 1 teaspoon baking soda, 1 egg, ¼ teaspoon vanilla, and 1 teaspoon cream of tartar; mix thoroughly. Grease pan lightly; press dough into pan. Bake in a preheated 375° oven about 15 minutes. Remove from oven and cool completely.

In a large bowl, combine one 8-ounce package softened cream cheese, 1 teaspoon vanilla, and ½ cup granulated sugar; beat until light. Spread cream cheese mixture over cooled crust. Arrange fruit such as sliced strawberries, grapes, kiwi slices, pineapple tidbits, banana slices, or peach slices on the crust.

In a medium saucepan, combine 1 cup orange juice, 1 cup granulated sugar, ¾ cup water, 3 tablespoons cornstarch, ¼ cup lemon juice, and ¼ teaspoon salt. Bring to a boil, stirring constantly until thickened; cool to lukewarm. Pour glaze over all; cover and refrigerate until serving.

Norma M. Sharratt
Tyler, Minnesota

BARN MURAL. Rosemount, Minnesota. Conrad Bloomquist, Scenic Photo Imagery.

Barn Murals Are Booming

Farmers now are more prosperous than they have been since 1919, and some of it they're spending on barn murals. The cash income for farms is much higher than it was in 1932, which was the trough of the depression. Farmers have been generous in buying war bonds, but a farmer's sock is deep and long and some of its content is going into outdoor art.

Here's something that helps: farmers can get paint for keeping up their houses and barns; so the barn artist does not have to worry about rationing.

Meet the king of all barn muralists: Frank H. Engebretson, Sr., Brodhead, Wisconsin. He has put more paintings on the outside of barns than any man who has ever lived. Around him and near him are more barn paintings than anywhere else.

He has always "dabbled in art," as he puts it, but it wasn't until 1914 that he painted his first barn mural. It is still standing and is in a fairly good state of preservation.

He has done 100 barn murals. An astonishing number. He says, "I never pass a handsome barn without wishing I could put a mural on it."

He says his finest is one on the J. M. Engebretson estate, near Wiota, Wisconsin. The title of the mural is "In the Rockies." He says: "I'll probably never do a better mural than that. People come again and again to see it. When they do that you can know you have put into it something that is pretty fundamental."

The average mural will run about forty feet in length. Now and then one gets up to seventy. But he has to his credit a veritable giant—a landscape 150 feet in length. It is on the Chapman farm, Woodford, Wisconsin. It took him five days to paint it. It is on the side of the barn; no ordinary barn would be that wide.

Most barn murals depict rural scenes; the favorite is a winding river; sometimes cattle are standing near.

Another favorite is the covered bridge. "People seem to like to hang on to the old," says Mr. Engebretson. "I have never had but one request to put in an airplane. As for myself, I don't care for an airplane in a barn painting. Just doesn't fit. If one were painting a hangar, or a shelter at a landing field, that would be different. Cows and rivers and windmills are better subjects for outdoor farm art."

The author of this article is something of an enthusiast for barn murals. Just how it started I don't know, but for years every time I saw a barn painting I stopped and basked. First, I loved farms. Second, I suppose I had a yen for art. Anyway, there it was.

Last year, as I was standing in front of my barn, near Maryville, Missouri, I thought of an early barn that my father had put up but which a cyclone had put down. I thought of his early days on that farm. In fact, he had come to that prairie section in a covered wagon drawn by an ox team. I thought: "There ought to be some kind of memorial to my father and mother arriving on this farm." I thought of having a painting made on my new barn that would commemorate their arrival.

I talked the idea over with an artist in my own town—Ellis Meek—who bore an excellent local reputation. He was astounded. A painting 36 feet across! And he didn't know anything about how a covered wagon looked; its details. Or how an ox-yoke looked.

Began the adventure of getting authoritative pictures of covered wagon days. I wrote to the studios in Hollywood and asked them to send me "stills" showing the details of ox teams and prairie schooners.

Ellis Meek and I worked out a water color sketch—the hardest thing of all to "get" was the mounted figure. My! The horse's head was not right; there was not the proper bend to the horse's forefoot. At last, everything was right, and Ellis started to work.

First, he divided the sketch into little squares, then the end of the barn into the same number of squares. These little squares on the water color sketch were enlarged sixteen times.

I tell you it was exciting, day by day, to see the painting grow! Five weeks it took, not a full day each time, for there was the problem of storm and light.

Finally came the day when it was done. I was the owner—the proud possessor—of a barn mural. But not just an ordinary, everyday barn mural (so I thought), for it showed my own father and mother—prairie pioneers. It is the only one of its kind in the United States.

Pennsylvania flourishes with barn murals. They are thickest near Doylestown. The closest barn mural to New York City that I know of is one in Dutchess County, hard by the town of Amenia, and is on the front of an old coaching inn, the Drovers' Inn. This shows a herd of cattle being driven along a rustic road. Take a look at it the next time you're out coaching.

Personally, I'd like to see every barn have a mural; especially if the painting shows some local scene. It seems to me this would be beautiful.

Originally printed in *The Christian Science Monitor Magazine*, January 29, 1944.

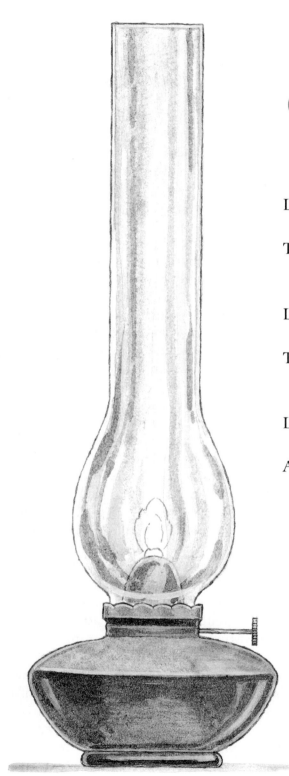

Oil Lamps

Gertrude Rudberg

Light up the old lamp, Mother;
    It's time that we came in
To the comfort of your kitchen,
    Where love lies deep within.

Light up the oil lamp, Mother,
    Way in the dining room,
To chase away the shadows
    And drive away the gloom.

Light up the best lamp, Mother,
    For guests may come tonight,
And we shall play the piano
    While we sing beneath its light.

Because of Your Love

Patricia Ann Emme

Sometimes it feels like summer,
Even on a winter day;
It happens when you smile at me
Or look a certain way.

Sometimes I feel the sunshine
When it's raining from the sky;
It happens when you hold my hand
And when I hear you sigh.

Sometimes it feels like heaven,
Where my every dream comes true;
It happens when you look at me
And say, "I love you, too."

Silvery Night

Susan E. DiVenti

The sun sets with a rosy glow
To change, from white to pink, the snow,
Which turns from pink to white again
As the moon rises over this verdant glen.

Majestic evergreens draped in lace
Stand demure in all their emerald grace,
And the mountains, tall, their crests bedight
With crystal crowns, on this silvery night.

Earth's canopy is adorned with stars,
And its ornaments—Venus, Moon, and Mars—
With wisps of Milky Way angel's hair.
What a wondrous delight earth and heaven share!

The night luster of this sylvan place
Is a joy that nature can embrace;
Tiny juncos and the snowshoe hare
Dance upon snowdrifts without a care.

But the wind and cold end their rendezvous
As the moon's veiled face takes a different hue
And the evergreens shake their branches clean
Of their silky garments of crêpe de Chine.

Now, a delicate, feathery flake from beyond
Alights on the glass of the mirrored pond,
And the silent snow falls soft and light
On this ethereal, silvery night.

Winter Serenity

Elizabeth Hobsek

So radiant is the moon tonight!
The brilliance of her mirrored light
   Deepens shadows on the snow;
   Silver diadems now glow
Upon Earth's gown of white.

How tranquil is our town tonight—
The hectic pace has taken flight,
   And in its stead, quiet reigns.
   I can see in windowpanes
Flickering candles bright.

As I enjoy this splendid sight,
A gust of wind, with pure delight,
   Snatches gems from Earth's gown fair
   Up into the frosty air
To crown the moon this night.

WINDOW OF DREAMS
Original art by Donald Zolan

WINTER ACONITES AND SNOWDROPS
Jane Grushow, Grant Heilman Photography.

Snowdrops and Winter Aconite

Quick. What's the earliest spring blooming plant you can think of? If the image of a crocus comes to mind, I wouldn't be surprised. These colorful little plants are popularly considered the first harbingers of spring. But what about the snowdrop? And the winter aconite? I think these two brave early bloomers have been shortchanged! Many people are completely unaware of their existence, which is a shame, because with them as part of the garden lineup you can have something in bloom just about all twelve months of the year in most parts of the country. Often appearing a full two weeks before the first crocus pokes its head up out of the muddy turf, the sunny yellow winter aconite (*Eranthis hyemalis*) and the pristine, delicate-looking snowdrop (*Galanthus nivalis*) make their first

appearance in February in northern climates, and in the South you can look for them in January.

It's no accident that the one plant has been named after Old Man Winter and the other is named after the snow in which it is often found blooming merrily away, regardless of the temperature. Maybe that's why they haven't received as much acclaim as the crocus: one resembles the crocus enough to be mistaken for it by the uninitiated, and the other, being the same color as snow, is easily overlooked. On the other hand, maybe people just aren't as tired of winter when snowdrops and winter aconites appear as they are a couple of weeks later when the crocus bursts onto the scene. As much as I like winter ski trips, ice-skating parties, and ice hockey, being a gardener, I crave any sign at all that spring is really on its way. These hardy little plants never fail to provide that reassurance.

Each plant has its own special appeal. What I admire about the snowdrop is its seemingly delicate blooms that faithfully reappear each year in the coldest weather yet never exhibit damage from the chill. I also like its modest, head-down appearance. As a child I was enchanted by the snowdrops in my grandmother's garden. They always made me think of a group of little bunnies praying together. Another attractive aspect of the plant is its blue-green foliage which lingers long after the blooms die.

If you like flowers that can be planted and forgotten, the snowdrop is for you. It needs nothing. Plant the bulbs in the early fall or late summer in a partially shaded location, and that's it. Snowdrops look attractive under shrubs or trees and along the edges of wooded paths. Just leave them alone, and they'll bloom like clockwork year after year.

No matter where you live in the Temperate Zone, snowdrops are one of the first blooms to appear. In the far North they will come up later than farther south, but you can be assured that once you see them, winter is on its way out the door. About the only place they won't do well is in the semitropical climates of Florida and the Gulf Coast, but if you live there you don't need to be reassured that warm weather is on its way back—it hardly leaves! The *Galanthus* family, which is a native of Eurasia, includes about ten species, of which only two are widely available for the garden. The largest is the *Gelwesii*, or giant snowdrop, hardy only to the northern United States and coarser in appearance than the diminutive *G. Nivalis*, or common snowdrop. The *Simplex* variety is a single-blossomed beauty, and the *Flore Pleno* is a larger, double variety.

The winter aconite is a plant that I didn't stumble across until I was an adult, and I literally stumbled across it in a friend's garden. At the time I exclaimed that I had never seen crocus blooming quite so early. My friend set me straight, and I decided that anything that bloomed before the crocus was more than welcome in my garden. The fragrant, yellow-bloom-ing winter aconite is actually a member of the buttercup family and is a native of Turkey. Unfortunately, commercial demand resulted in so many plants being dug in the wild that the species has become seriously threatened. Now nursery-grown bulbs from Holland are available, and you can help save the species by insisting on documentation of the origin of the bulbs you purchase.

Winter aconites, like snowdrops, will naturalize freely and, once established, will quickly spread. To encourage this, give them an environment in which they will be protected but not smothered. Unlike the crocus, the winter aconite does not enjoy being planted in the lawn. It does best in the bare ground under trees, in a shady rock garden, or along the edges of a shrub bed. Though considered a ground cover, it cannot tolerate heat, so the area in which it grows will be bare looking once hot weather arrives and the foliage dies. A summer mulch of shredded bark will protect the bulbs and disguise their habitat until the foliage reappears.

Snowdrops and winter aconites can both be planted in August, and like all small-bulbed species, if you plant them, plan on planting lots of them. They really need to be set out in great drifts to have an effective appearance. The easiest way to plant small bulbs like these is to dig out a long, wide area where the plants are to be located. Dig it a little over four inches deep and set the bulbs two to four inches apart. (Soak the winter aconite tubers in water for twenty-four hours before planting.)

Setting out hundreds at once will keep you busy for a few days in late summer or early fall but will also reward you with a spectacular early, early spring display of blooms. So, if you're battling the late-winter blues, think how nice it would be to look out and see low-lying clouds of bright yellow, sunny-faced winter aconites and pure white, bell-shaped snowdrops smiling back at you. Then find that garden catalog and start planning for next year!

Deana Deck lives in Nashville, Tennessee, where her garden column is a regular feature in The Tennessean.

The Surprise

Patience Strong

When I see a snowdrop,
I just have to stop and gaze.
This miracle that happens
In the worst of winter's days
Always takes my breath away.
I can't believe it's true.
It looks so frail and beautiful,
So fresh and white and new.

It steals into the world
Before you realize it's there.
When the skies are bleak and bitter
And the trees are bare,
Secretly the snowdrop
Comes to ring her fairy bell
Like some shy soft-footed stranger
With good news to tell.

SNOWDROPS (*Galanthus nivalis*)
LeFever/Grushow
Grant Heilman Photography

The Flower

George Herbert

*How fresh, oh Lord, how sweet and clean
Are thy returns! even as the flowers in spring;
To which, besides their own demean,
The late-past frosts tributes of pleasure bring.
Grief melts away
Like snow in May,
As if there were no such cold thing.*

*These are thy wonders, Lord of love,
To make us see we are but flowers that glide;
Which when we once can find and prove,
Thou hast a garden for us where to bide.
Who would be more,
Swelling through store,
Forfeit their paradise by their pride.*

Readers' Forum

Contributing Editor Lansing Christman reads to Hilda Morrow's fourth grade class at Inman Elementary School, Inman, South Carolina.

To the *Ideals* Crew:

Could I only tell you
    How much it means to me
To open up your magazine
    To these good things I see . . .

I see the prettiest pictures
    And read the loveliest prose.
And oh, the excellent poetry!
    Tears trickle down my nose,

As I savor every single thing
    That's printed on each page,
All finished by great artists
    And writers of every age.

Please! Keep it all a-coming!
    You fill me up with glee
As I open it to these things
    That mean so much to me!

Helen M. Glass
Otter Lake, Michigan

I thought you might like to hear about some publicity that *Ideals* received recently when one of your contributing editors, Lansing Christman, read to the children at Inman Elementary School in Inman, South Carolina.

I had Lansing come along with me to keep me company while I read to fourth graders at the school. After I finished reading I pulled out your February 1993 issue from my briefcase and told the students that I had brought along a surprise guest who would read to them from one of his recent works.

It totally took Lansing by surprise as well as the students. . . . Afterwards the students crowded around him asking questions about his writing career and seeking autographs.

I just couldn't let this recognition of your magazine pass by without telling you about it and especially since Lansing had the opportunity to bring his work to life for this group of youngsters. It was wonderful hearing him read so distinctly the lines he creates for *Ideals*.

Hilda H. Morrow
Inman, South Carolina

Statement of ownership, management, and circulation (Required by 39 U.S.C. 3685), of Ideals, published eight times a year in February, March, May, June, August, September, November, and December at Nashville, Tennessee, for September 1993. Publisher, Patricia A. Pingry; Editor, Lisa C. Thompson; Managing Editor, as above; Owner, Ideals Publications Incorporated, 565 Marriott Drive #800, Nashville, TN 37214. Stockholders: Simon Waterlow, President, and Martin Flanagan, Vice President, 565 Marriott Drive #800, Nashville, TN 37214. Known bondholders, mortgages, and other security holders: Egmont Foundation, VOGNMAGERGADE II, 1148 Copenhagen, K. Denmark and Sirrom Capital, 511 Union Street, Suite 2310, Nashville, TN 37219. Average no. copies each issue during preceding 12 months: Total no. copies printed (Net Press Run) 193,132. Paid circulation 31,080. Mail subscription 146,944. Total paid circulation 178,024. Free distribution 350. Total distribution 178,374. Actual no. copies of single issue published nearest to filing date: Total no. copies printed (Net Press Run) 149,290. Paid circulation 10,425. Mail subscription 136,229. Total paid circulation 146,654. Free distribution 110. Total distribution 146,764. I certify that the statements made by me above are correct and complete. Rose A Yates, Vice President, Direct Marketing Systems and Operations.

ideals®

50 Years of Celebrating Life's Most Treasured Moments